Medium Difficulty
Maze 1

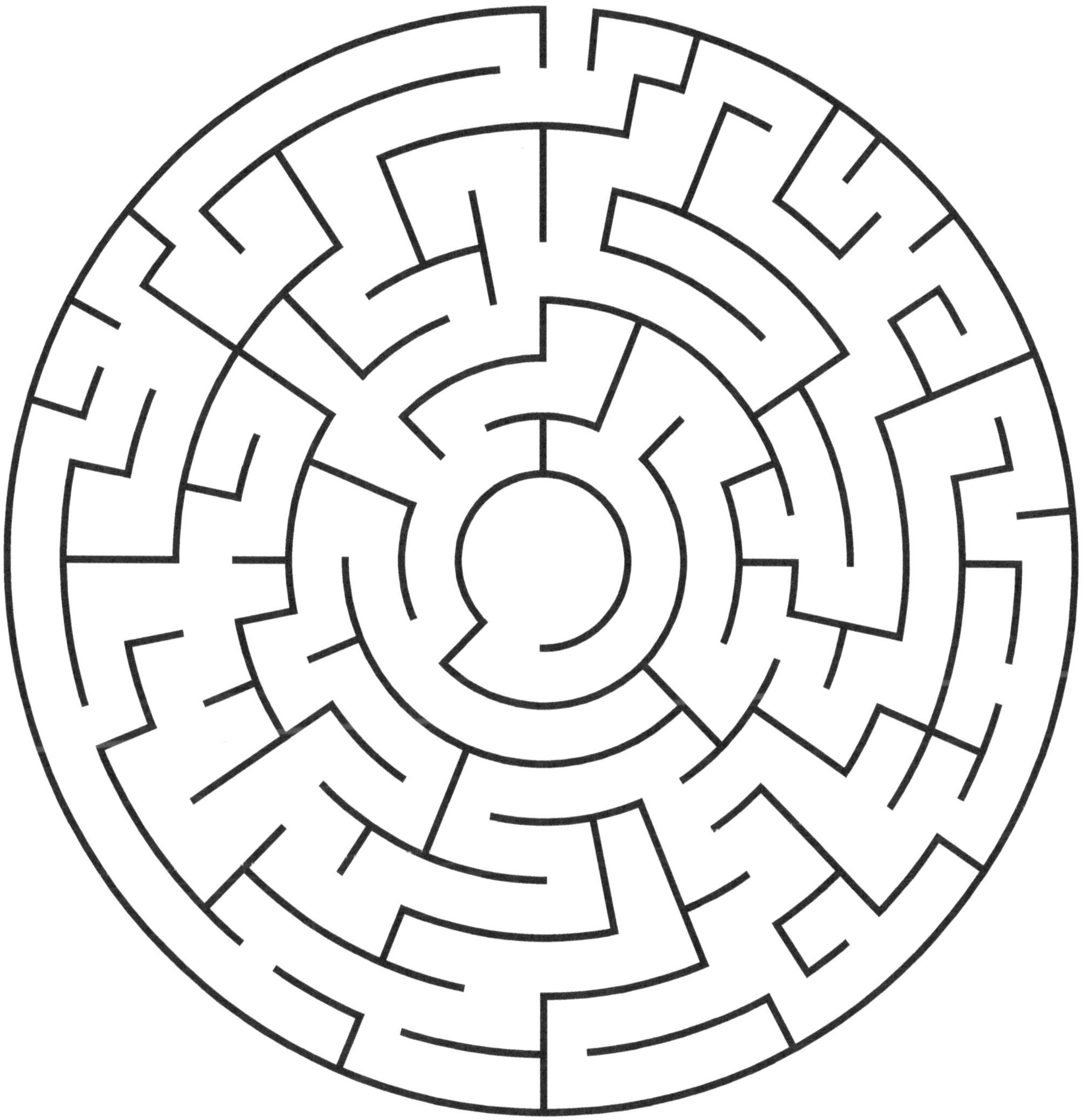

Medium Difficulty
Maze 2

Medium Difficulty
Maze 3

Medium Difficulty
Maze 6

Medium Difficulty
Maze 7

Medium Difficulty
Maze 9

Medium Difficulty
Maze 10

Medium Difficulty
Maze 11

Medium Difficulty
Maze 12

Medium Difficulty
Maze 13

Medium Difficulty
Maze 15

Hard Difficulty
Maze 1

Hard Difficulty
Maze 2

Hard Difficulty
Maze 3

Hard Difficulty
Maze 4

Hard Difficulty
Maze 5

Hard Difficulty
Maze 6

Hard Difficulty
Maze 12

Hard Difficulty
Maze 14

Hard Difficulty
Maze 15

Medium Difficulty
Solution 1

Medium Difficulty
Solution 2

Medium Difficulty
Solution 3

Medium Difficulty
Solution 4

Medium Difficulty
Solution 7

Medium Difficulty
Solution 8

Medium Difficulty
Solution 11

Medium Difficulty
Solution 12

Medium Difficulty
Solution 13

Medium Difficulty
Solution 14

Medium Difficulty
Solution 15

Hard Difficulty
Solution 1

Hard Difficulty
Solution 2

Hard Difficulty
Solution 3

Hard Difficulty
Solution 4

Hard Difficulty
Solution 5

Hard Difficulty
Solution 6

Hard Difficulty
Solution 7

Hard Difficulty
Solution 8

Hard Difficulty
Solution 9

Hard Difficulty
Solution 10

Hard Difficulty
Solution 11

Hard Difficulty
Solution 12

Hard Difficulty
Solution 13

Hard Difficulty
Solution 14

Hard Difficulty
Solution 15

www.ingramcontent.com/pod-product-compliance
Lightning Source LLC
Chambersburg PA
CBHW080923160726
48000CB00009B/3097